Hand in Hand Through the End of Life

TERRY LANIGAN, ACSW

*All the best
to you and your
family*

Terry Lanigan

ISBN-10: 1463695667
ISBN-13: 978-1463695668

DEDICATION

This book is borne of a daughter's gratitude for the wonderful and multi-faceted opportunity to accompany my mother through her old age, and ultimately, to her death. She had the good fortune to enjoy and appreciate life until it was her time to die.

To all those who have lost loved ones before it was their natural time to leave this life, I extend my very deepest sympathy. The complexity and depth of emotion that one experiences if death arrives as the "sad program of nature"—as my mother put it so well, is fundamentally different than the injustice one must carry if death arrives prematurely.

For those of us who have been lucky enough to have those we love with us through old age, and the resultant lifetime of experiences that we shared with them—I hope that this book will provide some level of preparation, insight, and support to walk hand in hand through the end of life.

ACKNOWLEDGMENTS

I would like to extend my appreciation to
the colleagues and friends who reviewed this manuscript with a
critical eye to the value of its content and the style of its delivery—

Thomas Moore, ACSW; Sheldon Eisenman, MD; Jo-Ann Kanter;
Caryl Malka; Patrice Cuddy; Amy Borgman, PhD; Sandi Metcalf;
Marianne Baran, RN

Finally, I would like to express my gratitude to Pamela Dazey,
without whom this book would never have come to publication.

CONTENTS

CHAPTER ONE

SAYING GOODBYE IS A FAR RICHER EXPERIENCE THAN SAYING HELLO

My mother died on Martin Luther King's birthday, 2009. She was diagnosed by her family physician to have advanced cancer exactly seventeen days before her death. She was 87 years old.

Some might say that this did not give her enough time to say goodbye to those she cared about. This is not true. In fact, my mother began the gentle process of saying goodbye to me many years earlier.

The neighborhood in which I grew up was predicated on the reality of traumatic goodbyes. My parents, and all of the adults that were part of my early life, were German Jews. These were people ripped from their homes, victims of a hideous reality of grief, loss, and traumatic separation from those they loved. There was no such thing as a loving goodbye. There was only survival, outrage, frustration, and confusion. I think that this is a universal experience when we are denied the opportunity to prepare for the emotion and changes in our life that come from loss. Obviously, the scale of injustice that people experienced as a result of the Holocaust far exceeds that which any given individual might be challenged by today. However, losing a child in a car accident, seeing a 30-year-old mother of three die of breast cancer, witnessing the death of a 20-year-old boy due to a brain aneurism … all of these horrific experiences bring up the emotions that were so often evidenced by others as I grew up.

Perhaps, this is why I feel such overwhelming gratitude to value a life-long relationship with appreciation and love, supported by a shared effort to prepare for the inevitability of death.

As I look back on it, I now get the picture that my mother began her process of saying goodbye to her lifetime of experiences by coming full circle back to her hometown of Heidelberg, Germany — and she took me along for the ride.

In early 2006, my mother, Edith, received an official invitation from the Mayor of Heidelberg to attend a reunion of Jews who had been forced to emigrate following the rise of the Nazi regime. As you might imagine, this effort at reconciliation was met with mixed feelings, but ultimately accepted, with me as her companion.

Her decision to return was not about her effort to come to terms with her past. It was about her effort to come to terms with her future. My mother was beginning the process of saying goodbye.

Prior to the rise of the Nazi regime, my mother often recalled a very good life for herself and her family in Germany. There were loving memories of her parents, sister, friends, continental travel, and cultural connection to her heritage. The pain that she felt being forced to say goodbye to that life—in acute crisis—was a trauma from which she never fully recovered. Although spared the horrific experiences of detention in a concentration camp, she often talked about the emotional upheaval that came with enforced displacement from her home.

Returning to the place of her childhood, after almost 70 years, was a form of closure for her that she allowed me to witness—a tremendous opening gift as she approached the end of her life.

During that wonderful week that we shared together, my mother was able to give me an unforgettable insight into the life that she had lived before I was born, before she was even an adult—influences that shaped the person that shaped me. In retrospect, this was the beginning stage of my unfolding capacity to say goodbye to her.

As my mother aged, I became keenly aware that she was no longer the person that she seemed to me to be when I was a child. To some extent, adulthood will do that to you. However, it was her old age that allowed me to become more attuned to the person she truly was—separate from her role as my mother. Our trip to Europe was, in many ways, a turning point in this recognition. We happened to have a fabulous time together—at 84, she was, and remained, far sharper in memory and capacity to enjoy the moment than I am now.

As we toured her home town, she showed me where she had taken piano lessons as a child—making sure that I knew the name of the instructor, the promenade where she and her teenage friends sunbathed on weekends, her bike route from school to home, the modern apartment building where she had lived with her parents and sister.

Memories of baby cousins who had been sent ahead to safety as Hitler rounded up the Jews ... as their parents wept goodbye, probably for the last time, were some of the painful stories that she recounted as we roamed the streets. As we continued our travels to nearby towns, we drove to a famous resort area—world renowned for its casino and mineral spas. As we walked in the gardens near the casino, we passed a small sign on the lawn with a cartoon picture of an adorable dog that said, "Dogs Forbidden."

My mother looked at me and said matter-of-factly, "The last time that I saw this sign it said: Jews and Dogs Forbidden."

I was struck by the tone of her voice. That tone communicated a realization that the sign in her mind was from a reality that was 75 years in the past—and that it was time to say goodbye to the world that was in favor of the world that is.

In addition to the local government of Heidelberg, this particular trip was sponsored by a Christian advocacy group named Bewegung, committed to an historical and emotional ownership and education of current generations about the devastating impacts of the prior Fascist political structure on the lives of innocent victims. Many of these good people maintained ongoing liaisons with Israeli officials and cultural emissaries, and my mother truly valued their heartfelt efforts.

Why was this fact important to the circle of life that I shared with my mother during the spring of 2006?

Because ownership of regret, self-evaluation, and honoring the experiences of those who have been wronged is a vital contribution to the richness of saying good-bye. The process may begin with the individual who is preparing to die, but it expands and balloons to all those around them after their death.

CHAPTER TWO

THE GIFT OF SUPPORT
FOR YOUR LOVED ONE
TURNS OUT TO BE A GIFT FOR YOU

In March 2001, I decided that I had to go on vacation. ANYWHERE. I had been divorced two years earlier and was raising my 13-year-old son on my own.

If you have ever lived in New York, you know that getting into a specialized high school is a process fraught with anxiety and stress for both parents and kids. Well, my kid got in. Great. But then, another type of stress began. The PTA. My mother told me, "Whatever you do, don't join the PTA!" I said, "Ma, the principal is being railroaded out. We have to take a stand in support of him. If we don't, who will?"

My mother, a 15-year member of the PTA when my brother was young, said, "Don't join the PTA. It is too much for you and they will drive you crazy." But, no … I didn't listen, and as you might expect, she was right. I attended two meetings and somehow ended up receiving 25 emails a day. Within two weeks, my stomach was bothering me constantly and I was trying to ward off daily headaches.

So, in January of that first year of my son's high school attendance, I called a travel agent and told her, "I don't care where you send me—this is when I want to go and this is how much I want to spend." So, with my parent's support and supervision of my son for one week, I ended up in Cancun, Mexico. It turned out to be a great vacation. Suffice it to say that one week in Cancun turned into a six-year long distance relationship, traveling between New York and Michigan—and by 2007—time for a decision.

My parents had lived in New York City since their arrival in the United States sixty-five years earlier. I had lived in the City for the past twenty years and raised my son there. Now, I was thinking of moving to Michigan. The first conversation was with my mother and father—85 and 87 years old respectively. How would they react?

They gave me a gift of approval. It would have been very easy and understandable were they to have pointed out that their advancing age was making day-to-day life more difficult. They could have pointed out that I would be giving up a quality of life that I had worked hard to achieve, with absolutely no guarantee that the decision would be in my long-term best interest.

But, they didn't. Both my mother and father talked about the life-long process of change, risk, and acknowledgement of new challenges. Their gift to me was the wisdom that these opportunities for personal growth continue through to the very end of life itself.

13

And, perhaps sooner than any of us expected, their commitment to this philosophy was put to the test.

With my son's approval and actual participation, I headed out to West Michigan on Memorial Day, 2007. I was concerned about my parents, but my brother lived nearby, and they were active in their neighborhood senior center, with many friends in the area. My plan was to return to New York every four weeks so that my parents would not feel abandoned, and I would not feel so guilty about moving away.

Within one month of my departure, my mother informed me that she wanted to see where I was living. "I would feel better if I knew what your standard of living looked like out there in the Wild West."

So, out she came. Although extremely well traveled throughout Europe, my mother had never been west of New Jersey, other than to visit me once during my graduate school years in Chicago. Years later, she would still tell the story of trudging through snow that was higher than the rooftops of the cars parked in the street, getting drunk on a little bottle of liquor she purchased on the airplane during her return trip to New York.

Edith had no idea what to expect when I picked her up at the Gerald R. Ford Airport in Grand Rapids, Michigan—six weeks to the day after I moved from New York. She arrived at the gate in a wheelchair. However, her face was beaming. My mother LOVED to travel.

It was midnight by the time we arrived at the house, but she was busy figuring out directions and taking in the different visual experiences of a summer night in the Midwest—alight until 10:00 PM.

There are lovely small towns that dot the Lake Michigan coastline, and we visited several that weekend. Lunches by the Grand River where the boats coasted down the Channel, window shopping in Grand Haven and Saugatuck, small resort communities with an artistic flair. She loved it. And then, she went home to New York. I was sad and she was sad.

On my return trip to New York the following month, my parents' anxiety about "the future" was more palatable. I learned something quite important. For all of us, the "well-elderly" are generally not fully well. And the needs continue to increase daily. Not just the acute needs. It is the chronic needs of your elderly parents that become prevalent in the lives of their adult children.

If your mother or father becomes seriously ill and an acute crisis ensues, an entire scenario unfolds over which you have little control.

For example:

At age 75, my mother fell in the downstairs hallway of her apartment building. I was living in Riverdale, about fifteen minutes away. At 7:00 PM, I got a frantic call from my father telling me that my mother had fallen and couldn't move. He had gone upstairs and dialed 911—an ambulance was on the way. I jumped into the car and arrived minutes before the ambulance. My only role was to talk to the EMT, sit with my mother in the ambulance as she was taken to the local hospital, and advocate for her insurance reimbursement while she was being admitted. Although stressful and important, basically, this was the beginning and end of my responsibilities in that acute situation. Obviously, visiting and support on her return followed. The chances are that most children of elderly parents will experience such a crisis at least a few times.

But, I am not talking about acute situations. The biggest responsibility lies in the chronic, ongoing needs of the elderly, and THAT is what my parents and I began to discuss during that return visit to New York in the autumn of 2007.

They talked about fundamental changes in their daily comfort, strength, and ability to navigate the details of independent living in a second floor apartment in the Bronx. My mother was tired. She had severe arthritis in her knees, making steps and hills up to the Senior Center increasingly difficult. Cooking meals was taking too much energy—shopping for food even more. The neighborhood coffee shop was a bus ride away, and it was hard for her to climb the stairs on the bus. The laundry room was outside the building on the first floor with two heavy doors to open, lock and unlock. The carpets needed a weekly vacuum and it was too heavy for her to push. A light bulb needed changing, but neither my mother nor father could get up on a ladder to change it. Besides, where is there a ladder in a Bronx apartment? They would have been scrambling up on a rickety chair. Food in the refrigerator got left for increasing periods of time because neither of them ate as much as they used to. Medical appointments were more frequent, but transportation to get there was a stressor in and of itself. My father's hearing and eyesight were rapidly deteriorating.

These were the issues discussed that afternoon. Both my brother and I had seen it, were concerned about it, but to hear my parents openly admit to these vulnerabilities and challenges added another dimension to the planning and decision-making process. It was not about the acute stuff—it was about the chronic stuff.

And the chronic stuff—day-to-day improvement in the quality of life had to be addressed. But how? They had lived in New York for so many years. They were socially active, although many of their friends were increasingly frail or had passed away. As Jews, New York was a familiar environment with refugees of all ethnicities—a critical mass of immigrants—throughout the City. Public schools are closed for Rosh Hashanah and Yom Kippur. Passover is as big as Easter.

In West Michigan? In the six years of my back and forth visits, I had met one Jew. ONE. And … he owned a blueberry farm. YOU'VE GOT TO BE KIDDING!

How in the world were my elderly parents going to make that kind of an adjustment? Even I, a woman in her forties, was a little freaked out by these cultural differences.

As my parents talked about the ways in which they were more challenged living in New York, future challenges of actually making a change to living somewhere brand new became part of the conversation.

And so, their gift to me in support of taking a chance to change my life and move with the flow of new realities became a gift to themselves. That day, the decision was made. I was going to start researching retirement communities providing appropriate residential options. My mother was going to schedule a trip to see them within two months.

The Search

It is intimidating to consider residential options for your elderly parents because the process confirms their increasing vulnerability. This is hard to accept, but important not to deny. The other risk in such an undertaking is to underestimate your parents need for independence, self-respect, and realistic capacity. The search is all about the non-biased evaluation of your parents' needs and the "feel" of the environment.

As in all serious pursuits, there is a science and an art to the process of choosing an appropriate living arrangement for your elderly family members. And trust me, it is both logistically and emotionally challenging.

The following issues comprise what I view as the "science" of your research:

- What level of support is available in the chosen community to address pre-existing medical needs?
- Potential future medical needs?
- Is emergency medical response available?
- Is the residence close to or isolated from stores, a library, movies?
- Would your parents need a car to take advantage of these resources?
- Is there a senior center nearby?
- Is there a well-run hospital nearby?
- Are there physician offices in the neighborhood for ongoing outpatient care?

- Is there a multi-phase-of-care philosophy exhibited in the retirement/assisted living community? Specifically, do you see progressive phases of care available based on need: independent living-----supported living-----assisted living----- nursing home.

- Are apartments and assisted living environments clean and well maintained?

- Is it affordable? When you consider this issue, remember that your parents may be facing increasing need for services, and you should be prepared for a two to three year window that may involve additional cost. It is always worthwhile to be aware of this upfront, because there may be a sizeable jump in cost between levels of care required.

- Is the living environment that you are considering close enough to your home so that you can be available, but far enough so that you can maintain some degree of physical and emotional distance? Personally, I experienced a big adjustment when I realized how quickly the adult child gets pulled into the whirlwind of elderly stress: Medicare bills, credit card errors, telephone disconnections, cable disruption, medication delays and so forth. There is a value in a little bit of physical distance from the eye of the storm.

The Art of the Research:
- Would your parents like their new home?
- Is the primary thrust of the services appropriate to your parents needs? (For example, both of my parents were

socially active, played bridge, engaged in political and historical discussions, and functioned independently. Assisted living environments are geared to more medically vulnerable populations, making that choice inappropriate for my parents at the time.)

- Is the administration philosophically in line with your own vision of a gentle environment to support your parents through their most vulnerable years?

- Is the staff warm? I don't mean courteous, I mean WARM.

- Are the other residents at the same level of independence or vulnerability?

- Are the other residents warm? I don't mean courteous, I mean WARM.

- Do you feel an underlying respect at the residence for the ebb and flow of later life?

These were the considerations and impressions that I engaged in. I use the word "engage" with purpose. One of the biggest differences between the well-elderly and the medically challenged elderly is that the former is a natural part of life that allows pro-active decision-making and a range of choice. Although there is anxiety faced by all members of the family as parents may move, have to leave old friends, and adjust to a new community, the overlay of acute deterioration and medical interventions is not paramount.

For those of us with medically challenged elderly parents, decisions are not proactive, but often of necessity, reactive. Adult caretakers face much more limited choice and greater emotional pain—all of the issues that must be addressed are interlaced with crisis, anger, and tremendous fear of the future.

I was lucky. I got to "engage" with my mother and share in the process of her conclusions. Being a social worker came in handy. I knew how to find resources, what to look for when I visited different senior communities, and how to interview administrators to elicit a "feel" for their philosophy and the quality of care.

Then came the next step—and the most decisive. My mother came to visit my top choices.

It was cold. I don't mean New York cold. I mean Lake Michigan cold. I had flown to New York to spend the weekend and fly out with her from the City to Grand Rapids. The entire swath of the U.S. from the East to the Midwest was in the midst of seriously wintry weather, and as we flew, my mother marveled at the lightening that surrounded us and turned the atmosphere above the clouds into an array of light show effects.

I was less appreciative.

We were the last plane allowed to touch down in Grand Rapids that night. Severe cold, snow and ice had cancelled hundreds of flights. My 80-year-old father-in-law was waiting for us at the gate, accompanied by his 25-year-old grandson. My mother was wheeled out of the airport in a wheelchair. Typical of a New Yorker, my mother tried diligently to tip the young man from the airline who pushed her in the wheelchair to the airport exit, but he refused to accept it. This was the first difference in attitude of many that my mom was to encounter in the near future.

ATTITUDE. Virtually every decision in life is based on your attitude. You can function so as to forestall loss—meeting all opportunities for a new experience with suspicion, anger, or regret. But there is another choice. To welcome change. To take a calculated risk. To dream about something new, even when you are 85 years old.

My mother chose the latter.

After she settled in at my house, she and I, basically, sat down for a business meeting. During the three days of her scheduled trip (she couldn't leave my father alone for longer), we plotted out three retirement communities that I had researched, visited, and determined might be the best potential fits. These were the facts that I laid out for my mother:

1. Name and location
2. My assessment of the advantages and disadvantages
3. My assessment of the 'community' philosophy
4. Resources available in each surrounding locale
5. Cost

I had scheduled interviews with each administrator for a tour of the living environment prior to my mother's arrival, ensuring that we would visit at a time when she could get a sense of the lifestyle and type of resident. From that point on, my mother took complete control. And she made it 100% clear to both me and the administrators that she was the sole decision maker in this scenario. You might expect that I would be thinking, "Well, of course, my mother and father are the ones going to have to live here—I am not a key player in this process." But, I was surprised at my own reaction. I had worked hard to establish the "appropriate" parameters for their new life. Would my efforts be devalued? Cast aside? Rebuked? Would she decide that such a new way of living was simply too great an adjustment at their age—and that they would be better off alone in New York? Would the resistance to change ultimately hold sway to cloud her current evaluation?

So, as we prepared for our first meeting the following day, these were the thoughts in the back of my mind. I had the notebook; my mother had a clear, concise outline of priorities in her head.

I was struck by the parallel experiences we confront at different developmental stages.

For a very young child, a parent must often make child care decisions. Part of that decision is based on the potential caregiver's qualifications: experience, education, and philosophy about child rearing. Part of the decision is based on the physical condition of her home or day care center. But the biggest factor is how the environment FEELS to you. What is your internal experience when you are there? Are you apprehensive, nervous, critical, uncomfortable, on edge when you visit? Do you find yourself looking for a way out, or wanting to stay? Are the people—even if they are children—in the environment relaxed and enjoying themselves? Do they reach out to you in friendship or for those very few minutes, do you feel shunned or disrespected?

Often, the way we do one thing is the way we do everything. Are these not the exact same issues that we address when we decide which college to attend, which partner to choose, which neighborhood to move to, and ultimately, which end-of-life environment to choose? Confronting the loss of the familiar, the perfectly normal fear of change, and the uncertainty of charting a new course is a process that we face at every major crossroad from infancy to death.

At every one of these crossroads, we can shun change and remain steadfastly grounded in our own comfort zone. My father always said, "The reality of life is that you are always making decisions. Even when you choose not to make a decision, a decision is made—and there is a price to be paid. You always pay a price." If you and your parents choose not to make any decisions, choose to avoid the inevitable challenges of the future, I would suggest to you that you are making a mistake.

My mother visited me on November 4. She made her decision. The retirement community in which she felt comfortable had five stages: condo living for the younger senior group, independent living in an apartment with a la carte support services (meals and cleaning help), "deluxe" independent living where the senior receives significant daily help (meals, daily housekeeping, laundry, medical transport), and finally, assisted living where residents live communally because they are no longer able to meet daily living needs such as taking medications for themselves, bathing, walking, and the like.

The biggest 'elephant in the room' when dealing with the needs of the elderly is an acknowledgement that life will get harder to cope with—even beyond the difficulties currently faced. Anticipating decline is an important factor to consider when researching and deciding upon the best environment for your elderly parents or loved ones. As well, if you are coping with a parent who is quite ill, physically disabled, or with serious confusion or disorientation, consider whether the environment in which they will live is really geared to providing the necessary services.

My ex-husband, a researcher, used to talk about statistical outliers—outcomes or events that fall on the lower curves of a normal bell curve of statistical probability.

You don't want your parents to be statistical outliers in their living environment. The level at which they function should be evidenced by the majority of seniors that you see. When my mother and I arrived at the 9:30 AM coffee hour at the Lakeside Villa Retirement Community, we were greeted by approximately 40 people, many of whom invited her to sit at their table. The talk was about bridge, their experiences in making lifestyle change, their enjoyment of this type of life in their later years, families, hobbies, and an acknowledgement by all that facing change has its good points as well as bad.

At the end of this breakfast get-together, an administrator came by to see how it all went and if my mother felt that she and my father could be comfortable living there.

There was a two-bedroom apartment available, which we had seen earlier that morning. In this sense, being from New York was a major advantage. As opposed to downsizing from a large home in a suburban neighborhood, my mother was thrilled that she would have a little terrace, two bathrooms and a washer and dryer IN the apartment!

Based on a handshake, my mother signed a lease on the dotted line. So ... my mother arrived for a visit to choose her future on

November 4. On January 5, my parents left New York together for the last time.

CHAPTER 3

"I'VE LEARNED MORE IN ONE YEAR
THAN IN A LIFETIME"

One of the recurrent themes that I have experienced in my life to this point is that there is a major difference between running away from something bad versus running towards something new. The former is generally an act of desperation borne of hopelessness and reaction. The intrinsic risk that defines change is not viewed in proper perspective because your actions are based on a fundamental precept—"ANYTHING must be better than the way it is now." This is often not true. Change should be modulated by your assessment of calculated risk.

There would be quite a few reasons for my parents to "run away" from their life in New York.

1.   Their apartment was in a typical six-story building located near a bus stop. In the past, this had been quite convenient,

but over the last several years, my mother could not climb the high steps on the bus, nor could she walk around downtown due to the pain of arthritis.

2. Although a superintendent of the building, with whom my parents had a wonderful relationship, lived downstairs, there were no support services in case of an emergency.

3. Their building was located down a hill in a very hilly section of the Bronx. The sidewalks were less than impeccably maintained, so the unevenness of the street created hazards to navigate—increasing their risk of falling.

4. The most direct access to their local grocery store was up a series of 100 steps. The alternative was climbing up a steep hill and around the corner.

5. Their neighborhood senior center was subject to drastic funding cuts. In my opinion, the single most devastating environmental influence for the elderly is isolation. The possible demise of this center suggested a future of unstructured time since many of their friends took a small bus to get there and would be unable to travel for a bridge game at their apartment independently.

6. Expense. For my parents to move to an assisted living residence nearby, they were looking at a monthly cost of $5,000 - $6,000. Clearly, this exceeded their financial resources and made the assisted living option in NYC a moot point.

So, there were many reasons to "run away." All of these issues were not enough to convince my mother of the need to move, however it did influence them to consider the VALUE of moving.

From the outset, my mother made it clear to me that the Michigan environment must be one in which they would experience a better quality of life because in many ways they were content—otherwise, they were not moving.

She was right. In retrospect, this was the only attitude that could forecast the foundation of their positive adjustment—THEY HAD A CHOICE. They were not running away. They were walking towards.

As my parents moved into their new apartment, I observed the similarities to what I had experienced when I moved away from home and into my own place—an experience that most of us have in our 20's.

Although my son and I fully unpacked all of their boxes the day of their arrival in order to decrease their sense of disorientation, my mother pretty much took over from there, with my help as a chauffeur. Just as with a young married couple, my mother took my father to assorted furniture stores to pick out new furniture and accessories for the apartment. They did not live out of boxes and suitcases, but committed to a new life that would be comfortable and as aesthetically pleasing as they could reasonably afford.

My mother had fun. She negotiated and bargained, made friends with salespeople, and used this initial process of adjustment as an avenue to interact with her new surroundings. One of the salesladies at a local furniture store came to pick them up by car to bring them to shop although their purchases were by no means excessive. She thought they were cute.

So, piece-by-piece, my mother, at the age of 85, organized a new life for herself and her husband. She established a social structure almost immediately. They had moved on a Saturday and attended the 9:30 AM coffee on Monday along with a bridge game. My mother called me a couple of times a day to inform me of their progress and nice opportunities emerged. In addition to very nice women, there was also a community of men, several of whom played bridge. This was wonderful for my father, who had lost his male card partners over the years and was often surrounded by women in the social activities that dominated their life in New York.

As my mother delved, quite purposefully, into an active social life for herself and my father, the cultural differences that I had anticipated that they would experience did emerge.

My parents had never lived in a house in their entire life. I have seen, myself, that men in the Midwest spend a huge amount of time talking about home improvements, mechanical repairs, and renovations. Growing up in my Washington Heights apartment, when a fuse blew it was a major catastrophe that enlisted the anxiety and helplessness of my father, fear of a full-scale blackout by my mother, and multiple feverish calls to the super who lived in an apartment in the basement. So, home improvement was OUT as a source of connection between my father and the other men in the community.

Sports. The other male pastime in Michigan is an almost fanatical commitment to both local and (rivalry based) regional sport teams.

Everyone knows the statistics of all of the players, the historical win-loss ratio of their teams, and argue strenuously about mismanagement steps of the coaches, scouts, and managers responsible for a losing season.

My father never cared nor ever will.

Establishing common ground is a challenge for all of us that are new to a community. Often, the best friends that one makes in adult life are with the parents of your children.

It is impossible to duplicate such friendships. No matter how much you enjoy or connect to a new friend, they do not share a 20 year, 40 year, or 60 year history with you. This was even more striking for my parents, as their traumatic experiences of childhood were totally foreign to the middle class, American-borne folks in their new residential community. But guess what? They were indeed able to make friends. The next-door neighbors in their new two-story apartment building were born in Holland, arriving in the U.S. in 1953. Another woman in the complex loved to shop at trendy stores along the Main Street, and Main Street reminded my mother of her hometown. As I watched my mother establish new relationships, I learned another very important lifelong lesson. We can choose to enjoy new people or we can choose to resent that new friends are not old friends. Acceptance that the past does not rule the future. It is your choice.

I believe that these were the perceptions that were prominent in her mind as she shared with me in one of our final conversations that she "had learned more in one year than in a lifetime."

CHAPTER 4

THE SOLACE OF ACTION

The eternal reality of the circle of life becomes more profound as your parents age. For many of us, a significant period of our early adulthood was devoted to raising young children. During infancy and early childhood, the demands are relentless—being intimately attuned to every period of their growth and development, efforts to protect them from harm, sensitivity to burgeoning emotional needs and interactions, sleepless nights of anxiety if the child is physically or emotionally upset. But, you always know that you are supporting a brand new life that is moving forward and upward.

The most seismic psychological shift when caring for your parents is coping with the overwhelming presence of the fact that your efforts at caretaking no longer support a movement forward and upward—but rather provide a cushion to their emotional and physical decline.

As a daughter, one of the most difficult caretaking tasks was to absorb the sadness that both my mother and father felt as to how restricted and encapsulated life becomes the closer you move toward death.

As valiant, and in many ways, successful as my mother was to pursue her social and intellectual life following their move to Michigan, the unavoidable limitations of her arthritis, gastrointestinal troubles, lack of mobility, and the pressures of supporting her elderly husband led to a painful frustration of acknowledging the limits that old age imposes.

The other feature that became ever more pronounced in my mother had less to do with the challenges she faced coping with her physical limitations, but rather, her emotional sensitivities.

As a child, I clearly remember the image of my mother looking out through our second floor window, with her body fully outstretched to watch for my brother coming home from the neighborhood school yard two blocks away. If my father missed his normal subway and came home from work a half hour late, my mother was already in tears, expecting that he had a serious accident. It was only now, when she was well into her 80's, that she recalled experiencing these high levels of anxiety even as a child.

At the age of five, Edith clung to her mother often and would cry when her father would come home late from work. Finally, after many weeks of her child's hysterical tears, my grandmother said, "Yes, so what if he is late? Do you think that he fell into a mailbox?"

These anxieties became heightened in her old age, with particular concerns about the entry-into-adulthood of my son. She called me every day to find out how he was feeling. Add this anxiety to my almost-neurotic efforts to be the best daughter (and best mother) that I could be, and my mother was making me feel like a nervous wreck.

As your parents age, "action" doesn't only mean doing things. It also means absorbing a great deal of uncomfortable emotion and underlying fear that your folks are experiencing themselves.

For my father, the issues were not overtly focused on anxiety about others—it was more about a tremendous frustration at an ever-increasing loss of personal control. My father had learned early on that independent survival was key.

Emotionally and physically, as a young person, my father was often alone. His mother had died when he was 16 after a lengthy illness, and his father was often away from home working as a salesman. His oldest sister had left for Palestine in 1933, when he was 14. By the time his mother died several years later, it was too dangerous for my aunt to return to Germany, so my grandfather insisted that she stay where she was. His elder brother and he shared little in common—both in terms of interests and temperament. Being socially isolated in his younger years because he was a Jew, and quickly realizing that he and his family would have to leave his home soon, my father—to the very last day of his life, put his emotions in his pocket and moved forward, doing what he felt needed to be done.

Therefore, as my mother became increasingly frail, he became increasingly insistent on maintaining control of details. Unfortunately, his hearing and sight had deteriorated significantly, leaving the expectation that my mother be his emissary for banking issues, telephone bills, resolving disputes with credit card companies, and the like.

My mother was not a detail-oriented person. My father's demands resulted in a great deal of anxiety and resentment, so I took on these challenges.

Hours spent on the phone, dealing with issues that are annoying even when they relate directly to me, totally overwhelmed my ability to cope. The next time that you pull out the credit card sized health insurance identification card, notice that it is almost impossible to read the phone number for questions and issues. Each ID number has approximately ten digits, and those numbers are not your social security number.

I have never been calm and in control when confronting bureaucratic incompetence. However, when trying to negotiate these things for my parents, I found two fundamental differences. The first was to realize that often, after lengthy waits on the phone to FINALLY speak to someone about a phone bill, moving expense, credit card error—the person on the other end of the phone, when you finally got them—wouldn't even speak to you because, "You are not the person on the account!" I cannot tell you how often I tried to explain that my parents were almost 90, and simply unable to deal with the upset and need for specific details required to resolve a problem. Often, actually nearly all the time, I would slam down the phone and dissolve into tears. Partly, because I had not been able to resolve the problem and partly, because I knew that I had no choice but to do it again.

An important piece of advise for adult caretakers; have your name listed on every telephone account, credit card account, television bill, and so forth. Make sure that you go through the legal process of power of attorney for both banking and medical statements. If your name is on the account, all of these companies and businesses will speak with you to resolve problems. If your name is not on the account, they won't. And then you face two problems:

1. Lack of problem resolution, and
2. Increasing anxiety from your parents that the problem isn't solved yet.

In many ways, these pressures took one of the greatest tolls on my emotional stability as an adult child responsible for the well being of my parents.

Unlike being a parent to a young child, the adult caregiver always has two roles to play. The first is as arbiter of the daily frustration noted above, but the second role is that of outwardly calm support as decline enfolds your parent's experience.

Being able to resolve problems of everyday life for your parents provides a safety cushion to them that is not to be undervalued. Aggravation is everywhere, but for the elderly, interruption of health insurance, medication, television hook-up, telephone access and the like are serious complications that easily spiral out of control as they confront their own helplessness to solve problems that, several years ago, would have been taken care of without anyone else's involvement. This fact can leave them depressed and resentful ... all emotions that the adult child is left to struggle with.

My parents had always maintained a cemetery plot in New Jersey—where all of their family who had escaped Europe were buried.

After living in Michigan for six months, my parents learned about a VA cemetery recommended by my mother's cousin who had transplanted to Ann Arbor several years earlier.

My mother and I went to investigate together. I must say that, initially, I was less than pleased to take the three-hour trip. I had been feeling somewhat pressured by other details and was just coming down from the high intensity of the move itself.

But, I am glad that I did, my mother liked it. We talked about the excellent maintenance of the property, respectfulness of staff, and what painful feelings she might have if she was not to be buried next to her parents. We talked about the specifics of what would be involved when she and my father died—realistically and calmly—and then went out for lunch before returning home. Although these conversations are not easy to have with your elderly parents, I strongly encourage you to do it. You are not talking about anything that your parents don't know is coming, and they have the right to have as much control of their end of life as possible.

When the time came to see my mother buried in this cemetery, I felt some solace in having shared the preparation prior to this time with my mother when she was active and felt pretty well. There was no panicked reaction to transporting the body back to New York, how to hold a funeral and shiva there—how my father could possibly tolerate that whole scene. My advice to you in this regard is: respect your dying parents' wishes and know your own limits. Discuss them openly with your parents while they are alive.

Know the limits and wishes of the surviving parent. Prepare for as much in advance as you can because there is only so much that you can emotionally and logistically handle when your parent dies. Because my mother had allowed me to walk through this process with her, before a crisis, her burial was as dignified as her death.

CHAPTER 5

DO EVERYTHING YOU CAN,
AND KNOW WHEN
EVERYTHING YOU CAN DO ISN'T ENOUGH

A few days after my mother was diagnosed with terminal cancer, we were sitting in her den and talking about my view of the thin line between life and death. I have had two 'visits' in my lifetime from people who had passed away—my grandmother and the deceased mother of my best friend. These dream-like experiences were life changing to me, and have totally altered my view of the line between life and death.

My mother, however, talked about having had nightmares for a year after my grandmother's death—thinking that she had forgotten to answer her phone call or pick up her mail. Somewhat callously (in retrospect) I said, "Well, you must have had some issues." She coarsely snapped back, "No, I didn't."

I didn't think much about this conversation until I woke up the next morning and realized why my mother might have felt this way. Now, I am very sorry for the brusque comment that I made.

My grandmother went into a large teaching hospital in the Bronx after she was diagnosed with colon cancer at the age of 80. Although she read the New York Times every day, the spoken language was more difficult for her, particularly with the many accents to be found in New York City. I now remember clearly how panicked my mother was on one of her return trips from the hospital.

My grandmother, fatigued and lying in a bed in a four-person room, had been instructed to take the pills that had been set out on the tray in front of her. Either she had misunderstood the instructions or the nurses made an error, but my grandmother DID what she was told—she took those pills. Apparently they were the wrong pills—as she was whisked off to Emergency to have her stomach pumped. To make matters infinitely worse, the doctor on call brought in a psychiatrist to evaluate why my grandmother was trying to kill herself. My mother had been visiting my grandmother at the hospital every day, but that was simply not good enough to avoid an event of such drastic proportions. It is only now, seeing the experience of a daughter's sense of responsibility first hand, can I image my mother's horror, anger, and sense of guilt ... for not being able to do enough.

When I was at the dentist recently, the technician briefly stated her experience attempting to care for her father the best that she could after her mother's death. After many independent years, the decision was made for him to be admitted to a nursing home.

Unfortunately, he was abused in that particular setting and as they awaited transfer out, he begged his daughter to stay each night and sleep on the floor, although the culprit had been identified.

What do you do in that situation? There was no other bed in the room; she had to go to work everyday. She did everything that she could possibly do. However, when she informed her father that she couldn't sleep there, her best simply was not good enough ... even though her intention was of the highest caliber.

The following statement is painful to say and painful to know.

It is never enough.

Ultimately, you have no choice but to realize that the big picture is out of your control.

INTENTION. Through our entire lives we are confronted with the disparity between our best intention and actual outcome. Sometimes, when we are lucky, the outcome matches our intention. As a young high school student, a kid can work diligently to obtain good grades, high test scores, and excellent references in order to be accepted at an elite university. Sometimes it works. Euphoria.

But sometimes—more often than not—factors outside of anyone's control determine the outcome. Legacy, affirmative action, financial limitations, geographical quotas, an autobiographical essay viewed with disdain, a bias against the high school by one of the members of the admissions committee—all these factors and dozens more can thwart all of the best actions by that student to achieve her goal.

And that dissonance between what we work so hard to create and what actually happens precipitates an array of strong emotion and behaviors.

GUILT. Feeling guilty for the dissonance between intent and outcome is my personal strong suit. For me, as I would venture to guess, for many, particularly women, the anger inherent in the experience of disappointment and frustration becomes internalized as an anger turned against yourself. Realistic lines of observation as we view our parents' decline and increasing dependency get blurred by the frantic effort to 'make everything right again.' Our intention and ultimate failure is the effort to re-stabilize an inherently unstable situation.

ANGER. Personally, I found that the anger that I experienced in my efforts to stabilize the increasing challenges and emotion-laden needs of my parents got directed at the external institutions with which I came in contact. Medicare, Social Security, the telephone company, the cable company, the banks ... it continues to astound me that our society makes absolutely no allowances for the limitations of the elderly. Therefore, for much of the year prior to my mother's death, I was often angry whenever a new issue came up. Not because of the issue itself, but because of the bureaucratic nightmare that I knew would ensue as a result.

TAKE YOUR TIME. Occasional procrastination is an interesting response to these pressures. I have always responded to all expectations as quickly as I could. However, there are actually times when taking a "breather" is an important tool to regain your composure and focus. This may be true not only regarding ongoing oversight of your parent's chronic needs, but emotionally as well. A game plan that includes brief respite from the responsibility is extremely helpful. Becoming resentful of your parents due to factors beyond their control does not improve the quality of their life—just the reverse.

PERIODS OF OVERWHELMING SADNESS. Part of doing everything that you can (and realizing that may not be enough) is acknowledging that the emotional support that your mother gave you as you were maturing from a child to an adult is no longer HER priority. I experienced a lot of loss around this developmental reality. Although she remained curious and aware of my life experiences, there was a shift to the lessons she had to teach about the process of dying. Whereas earlier in her life, the broad stroke of conversation was about ME, within five years prior to her death, the broad stroke of the conversation was acceptance of what was yet to come for HER. That was a developmental clash and my childish selfishness was present. I missed the focus being on me and her pride in me. Although embarrassing to admit, I think that this is a challenge and loss that we, as adult children, all face together.

Events became more rapid after the terminal diagnosis my mother received. We can never know the interplay between psychological and physical factors, but within two days of receiving the news, my mother was on an oxygen machine and taking increased doses of prescribed pain medicine. She contacted hospice at 3:00 in the morning, and received in-home services every day for a week. Nurses, social workers, volunteers, and a daily evaluation process for adult care and referral to the hospice center created a huge amount of comfort for both my parents and myself. Her anxiety diminished, as she knew that someone was always there to help her. We talked about the alternative that we most probably would have experienced in New York—calls to overworked physicians who didn't have time to return the call until hours later, long waiting times in an emergency room, a brusque and dismissive attitude by receptionists and insurance gate keepers, difficulty finding parking when I got them to the emergency room, possibly in the middle of the night, and most important, an overwhelming feeling that the professionals around just didn't care.

Eight days after my mother was diagnosed, she informed me that she wanted to go into the hospice house. I received a call from the hospice nurse who had been working with my mother for several hours as Edith insisted that she wanted to be admitted. The nurse told me that my mother's vital signs where stable and although she seemed very anxious she felt that, objectively, there was no need for immediate admission. Nonetheless, she made it clear to me that it was totally my mother's decision. I called my mother at home to ask her whether she was overreacting, having an anxiety-based reaction. My mother made it clear to me that she wanted to go into hospice immediately so, I said ok. We are simply not in the position to know the experience of others, and as adult children, we must maintain an underlying respect for the decisions that our parents feel that they need to make.

And, as it turned out, she was right. She was in hospice for a grand total of five days before she died.

On Sunday, January 18, there was a terrible blizzard. It was scary driving to the hospice. The last few days had evidenced her physical decline—she was awake less of the time each day, the pulsation of her carotid artery was increasingly prominent, and you could hear a rumble as she breathed.

Ironically, when I arrived on that day, a lovely volunteer was talking to my mother and feeding her a yogurt. My mother was fully oriented as she chatted (to the best of her ability) with this woman who had lived for several years in Fort Lee, N.J., where my brother currently resides.

My father and brother arrived very shortly thereafter and my mother fell asleep—on and off for several hours. Other than an oxygen tube in her nose to facilitate her breathing, there were no tubes, no IV's, no monitors. She was dying in a quiet, safe warm room with hand made comforters, a scene through the window of heavy snow falling, surrounded by her family, and a gentle caring staff.

At 4:00 PM, I said to her that I would see her tomorrow—she was semi-conscious. Just for purposes of chatting, I said that I would expect to watch Barack Obama's inauguration with her—that I thought it was scheduled for Tuesday, but I had understood from a brief snatch on TV, that it would be held tomorrow, Monday—and I was confused. She opened her eyes and said the inauguration was on Tuesday. Then she said, "be careful." These were the last words she said to me. I had to smile to myself to think that on my mother's deathbed, she was more fully oriented than I was.

I left her hospice room while my father and brother remained for another couple of hours.

When I left my mother that Sunday prior to the inauguration I knew that all of my emotional and intellectual energy had to be focused on preparation for what to do when I received the inevitable phone call from hospice. I knew that they would call me, and I would have to call my father and brother—my brother being quite unprepared for the rapidity of our mother's demise—he had come to Michigan for a few days on a planned visit. Although we could all see how quickly my mother was allowing for her own passing, I felt consumed by details: What was the best course of action for my brother to follow, how would I schedule my father's daily visit to hospice when he did not have a car, how could I schedule clients never knowing when the phone call informing me of my mother's imminent death could come at any moment?

These were the thoughts running through my mind that didn't allow me to sleep that Sunday night.

At 3:30 AM the phone rang … I knew why.

The hospice nurse had a voice as calm and clear as the sun piercing through the clouds. She said that my mother was showing the signs that death was very near and that the family may want to come and be with her when she died. Her voice calmed my inner chaos—her gift to me towards my mother's end was that of acceptance and lack of fear—my mother's view of the "program of nature."

I felt an array of emotions when I hung up the phone. Frightened, sad, agitated, physically attacked as if someone had punched my stomach, but all cloaked in a sheath of calm. I called my brother on his cell phone—no answer, so, I called the hotel, asking them to knock on his door for an emergency. Thankfully, they followed through and my brother called me back within a few minutes. With absolutely no logic at all, we debated whether to call my father. In hindsight, I wonder how we could have even questioned the decision, but in the heat of the moment, our own fears were displaced on to my father—fears that we couldn't handle watching her die—how could he, at 89, possibly make it through the experience? But of course, within five minutes we agreed that my brother would call him, pick him up, and we would all meet at my mother's room as soon as we could.

Although the snow had stopped the day before, drifts were high and driving remained treacherous. Nonetheless, I felt calmed by the half hour drive to reach my mother.

Evidently, not so for my brother and father. When I arrived at 4:30 AM, they were not there yet, but should have arrived before me.

The hospice was well lit and warm, with calm alert staff to help prepare me for what I would soon witness. Still no brother and father. Where WERE they?

I called my brother on his cell. He answered with an anxious voice. His car had gotten stuck in a huge snow bank nearby—he had no idea of the street they were on as all of the street signs were covered in snow and it was 4:30 in the morning. He couldn't even call the police for help because he didn't know where he was. I sat in my mother's room, watching her breathing become more erratic thinking about what it would mean for everyone concerned—my mother, my father, my brother ... and me, if they were not present for her last breaths.

Contrary to my expectations, they had managed to pull the car out of the snowdrift and they arrived at 4:45 AM. They settled in and I got coffee for us all. My mother was calmly sleeping—although she was snoring loudly. The hospice nurse explained that as death approaches, mucus and other fluids build up in the lungs, and this is what we were hearing. She prepared us to see my mother's breath slowing, become more erratic, and finally ... stop.

My mother died at 5:53 AM.

I will be forever grateful that my mother died not having to spend the end of her life in a hospital. The caring, understanding, and amazing competence of both in-home and in-center hospices care teams simply cannot be overstated.

CHAPTER 6

BEING EMOTIONALLY PRESENT WHEN YOUR PARENT DIES

You know, within a few days after my mother's death, I found that the outline for all of these chapters in this book were very clear in my mind. I was overwhelmed by the weave of emotional disorientation and intellectual clarity that I felt. To my surprise, when I started to put pen to paper, it all followed the path.

But it is not until right now that I see how my superficial intellectual clarity disguised the most important aspect of walking hand in hand through the end of life.

BE THERE. Sit with your mother or father. Talk. Talk about the three most important things so clearly laid out by Dr. Ira Byock—thank them for what they gave you. I apologize for how I let you down. Acknowledge with love your acceptance of the mistakes that they have made, if that is part of the inner struggle for you.

I was lucky. Both of my parents always made it clear to me that they were trying their best and that mistakes are an inherent part of living life and being a parent.

For me, the depth of emotion was based on sharing my thanks and appreciation to my mother. And again, I was very lucky. My mother was in and out of consciousness for the last few days of her life, but when awake, she was fully oriented and aware of her surroundings.

My mother was a big crier—as I am. My son can attest to that. I cry when I experience a wide range of emotion, as did my mother.

As I sat with her alone in her hospice room, I shared with her how much I appreciated all of the lessons she had taught me throughout my life. How very much I had enjoyed our vacation together, how much I valued her support as I was raising my son. The tears were rolling down my face as I held her hand. And you know what? She was smiling and squeezed my hand tighter. Her reflection of my appreciation gave her joy as to how she had been successful and made such a strong contribution to me, not the reflection of any sense of her sadness, loss, or denial of what was to come.

She was able to say to me, "I know how sick I am, but I am happy." Just as my mother gave me the gift of acceptance and support when my life began, she did the same for me as her life ended.

A few days after my mother's death, my son showed me a midnight email that my mother had written to him a few days after her diagnosis—less than two weeks before her death. I have included it here:

My darling Alex,

It's late at night and I can't sleep. I am remembering when I was your age. It was 1943 and all the boys were in the army and no one had a date. Things looked so hopeless with no end of the war in sight. How strange the things one remembers. Now you are 22. Live your life. Find someone to share it with. Do a little kindness everyday. Help a little old lady across the street. Engage the shyest girl at a party in conversation. And give an extra quarter to the poor guy at the corner and you will find that your own day is brighter.

I hope you will get your wish to go to medical school, but there are many ways to get there.

I am beginning to ramble and should get back to bed.

Grandpa himself is not well and I have to be careful with him. He has been diagnosed with a severe heart condition.

It is sad that things have come to this, but we are old and it is the program of nature.

We had a wonderful year here in Michigan and met many wonderful and caring people.

Most important, we have our family, whom we love so much and are so proud of and in the final analysis that's what counts.

Keep well my love, I will always cherish every moment we had together.

Grandma

No one was more emotionally present during the approach of death than my mother herself.

I guess the most challenging part of being emotionally present as you witness your parent's death is sitting with the tremendous emotional and intellectual disorientation that you feel. This is very hard to explain. In Yiddish, there is a term called "vermischt." Being vermischt means that it is hard to focus, your priorities are in flux, concentration is fleeting, and you feel generally confused.

So, being emotionally present while she was dying was enabled by the fact that my mind did not have to panic about logistics. There were no decisions left to be made, no frantic efforts to compensate for previous avoidance.

I could sit with my mother in peace.

And this is how it happens. My girlfriend, Caryl, had said to me that when her father died, she could almost see the spirit leave the body. I understood this as I sat with my mother for a few minutes after she stopped breathing. The face was hollow; the skin stretched across her face became almost immediately tighter.

But I talked with her and said goodbye as if she was there hovering above me.

Because—take a chance—if there *is* a period of transition from one life on the planet to a different level of consciousness—make the most out of the time in between. Share that time with the hope that you are being heard and loved.

How do I describe the feeling of gathering up her things and going back to my parent's apartment after my mother's death?

The most truthful thing that I can say is that I felt like a balloon with a slow leak in it, that eventually had no air left. That is how I felt.

CHAPTER 7

HEALING THE FAMILY

It can go either way. In my case, it went the right way. My brother and I had grown up very close. I have many memories of him taking me along to his activities ... probably, having a baby sister around was also a good conversation starter to meet girls.

There are eight and a half years between my brother and myself. My mother had been diagnosed with a dangerous tumor at the age of 29, and was strongly advised to hold off having another child for at least five years. So in many ways, I was quite spoiled by everyone, including my brother.

I was 10 years old in 1968. My brother was almost 19. He is currently a full professor in political science, and has received a Lifetime Achievement Award from the American Political Science Association. But at the time, I got to go to cool SDS meetings, Christmas dinners at varied girlfriends' houses, and a valued position as an evaluator of new girlfriend prospects. I knew many of his friends, and he would bring me along for Sunday night pizza or Friday afternoon malteds with pretzels at the local soda shop.

As I became an adult our relationship changed. He was embarking on a challenging, successful career. I had gotten married out of graduate school and lived in Chicago and Boston, until the birth of my son seven years later. Throughout that period, we would get together periodically and we all had fun together.

But later, with the many decisions, responsibilities, and challenges we face as "advanced" adults, we grew apart. Quite a bit. And it was painful all around. I think particularly for my parents—but there was nothing to be done. It was what it was.

When I visited New York in the early days after my move to Michigan, I rarely saw my brother. Over the twenty years during which I had made many friends, and between visiting them and spending time with my parents, there never seemed to be a convenient opportunity.

My parents and I discussed their consideration of a move to Michigan without my brother being around, yet my mother was particularly concerned about his reaction—they were very close.

So, I heard through my mother about the conversations she had with Stephen. He was initially concerned but gave them a full go-ahead the following day. Thereafter, my brother and I shared several phone calls to confirm that this would be a good decision all around. This was all fine, but soon, the difficulty was to begin.

Preparing for changes in Medicare coverage and required documentation. Scheduling the moving company. Coordinating moving dates with the administrators of the retirement community. Overseeing change in mail addresses. Cable. Telephone. Newspaper. Making arrangements in the new apartment for all of the above. Being present for the arrival of the movers. Buying all of the necessities to facilitate a comfortable arrival. Unpacking all of the boxes. Taking my mother shopping for furniture. Scheduling furniture delivery. Going to the new bank. The list could go on for another few pages.

And I was starting to find out—let me prepare you—the freak-out is again, quite similar to experiences as a new parent. It isn't due to any one thing, it is the accumulation of many tasks, which you would prefer not to be doing, compounded by the stress of responsibility.

And my brother, who called my parents every day, was back in New York … not responsible for any of this oversight and direct responsibility for a smooth transition.

At the time, I was frustrated that he had it easy and I was doing all the work, but as my mother approached the end of her life, I realized that he experienced a very strong emotional burden and sense of loss due to his **absence** from the process that I had gone through together with my parents.

For me, it was this realization that melted many emotional walls that I had built over the years. As she got sicker, my brother's truly heartfelt appreciation for my efforts, and his sense of loss for not being able to share the last year of our mother's life with her … this had a profound effect on my emotional connection with him as the beloved sibling of my childhood.

My brother had been coming out to visit my parents every six weeks or so. As I had mentioned earlier, his trip in January had been planned with the intention of visiting my mother a little sooner due to her diagnosis. I remember the telephone conversation when I told him the result that the doctor had shared with me, that I had in turn, shared with her.

"You didn't tell her … don't tell her (about the diagnosis)," he said.

I bristled.

"Of course I told her—she's not stupid, she's 87 years old, and she was the one that basically told me that the situation 'was bad' before she even had the tests."

"You shouldn't have told her."

I was upset. The message that I heard, as a caretaker of primary responsibility was, you didn't do it right. But I quickly realized that was not the message that was going through my brother's mind.

He didn't want to allow my mother to believe she was going to die.

My mother knew that she was going to die. I felt that holding a secret from her was not the answer.

To this day, I do not regret the honesty of full disclosure. My mother and father had the right to know and to prepare.

Now, the argument can be made that my mother "gave up" after finding out that she had advanced cancer. After all, she died approximately two weeks following diagnosis.

However, of all of the decisions made over the prior year regarding my parents' well being—I am firmly convinced that this was the best and most important decision of all. Ultimately, it was clear to me that neither her doctor nor I told her anything that she did not already know.

It could be said that her will to live diminished, shown by her immediate request for in-home and center-based hospice.

But, she had been preparing to let go for many months prior, and now, was peaceful as she allowed the "program of nature" to unfold.

Stephen changed his airline tickets to come in the following week.

But, his understanding of me and my true acceptance of his appreciation only really felt authentic to me beginning that weekend. HE KNEW. He could see the excellent service and high caliber of the hospice, but more importantly, he FELT the emotion and shared in the responsibility of preparing my father for our mothers' death— as well as sharing this most poignant of life experiences with my mother.

That weekend, my brother and I truly shared the role of adult caregivers to our parents—and it melted years of emotional distance between us.

We talked about our childhood, the special and distinct relationships that each parent shared with us—he as the first-born, me as the baby, family perspective, and sibling rivalry.

My mother and brother were very close. Stephen was hit very hard as he watched our mother dying.

And he was truly grateful to me for enabling them to live a high quality life until the end. As often as he had said it in the past, it felt totally different to me to be one family together and feel what he had been trying to say.

My mother's death brought about a profound healing of my relationship with my brother—an amazing opportunity to create in the present what my mother had so dearly fostered and nourished in the past. Another final gift.

CHAPTER 8

THE ROLE OF SPOUSES

My life partner grew up in the Midwest. Ken doesn't talk much about things out of his control.

New York Jews **always** talk about things out of their control—health, politics, other peoples' relationships, expectations for their children, perceived insults ... the list can go on and on. I am pretty classic.

I talk to my friends, my colleagues, my relatives, and all relevant professionals at a time of emotional stress. When a crisis like this strikes ... Ken renovates.

He measures, he hammers, and he polyurethanes—he builds.

Virtually all of his coping style is non-verbal—at least about the things that are out of his control.

So, I found myself questioning my expectations of him. Can you ever expect your spouse to provide a supportive environment to you with tools that are not theirs—but are yours? And ultimately, the reality is that all your spouse can do—is to provide a supportive environment—because these are your parents, not theirs. The emotions—fear of loss, frustration, helplessness, are only fully felt by the person facing their own parent's end of life, no matter how caring and concerned your partner may be.

So, I found myself going through various stages with Ken. Initially, as I struggled with all of the details of their move to Michigan and efforts to stabilize medical insurance, telephone, address changes, etc., I felt a certain resentment of his emotional and functional detachment from the whole process.

It took some time, but I finally realized that I was not resentful of Ken. I resented the battles with the outside world. Resentment turned to frustration. That frustration may have been played out on my spouse, but on a very deep level, it was grounded on the reality that despite all of my very best efforts, I could not halt or even stabilize my parent's decline that was staring me in the face every day.

The night that I received the phone call that my mother was close to death, Ken woke up as well when the phone rang. As I noted, the hospice was a half hour away and a blizzard had tapered off the night before. He asked, "Do you want me to drive you?"

Inside, I was livid. "What the hell do you think I want you to do, you ***" was the line running through my head.

I said, "Yes, I want you to drive me," but he didn't really move to get up. So, I gave it a minute and when there was no further movement I said to myself, "Fuck this," but on the outside said, "You don't have to go, I'll go myself." I felt like a martyr as I turned the key in the ignition. A lot of resentment was flowing through my head.

But, I was surprised.

As the light changed from red to green on the road, the resentment lifted. I realized that this was a very personal experience for me and my family of origin. I focused on breathing and emotional preparation for her death during that drive to the hospice.

Rather than conversation about what I was feeling, I allowed myself to prepare.

And this preparation was even more poignant as my father, brother, and myself sat at my mother's bedside. I was experiencing the death of a woman that Ken had never met—the mother of my youth.

For him to be present with my family of origin would have been an emotional intrusion.

After she died, we went back to my parents' apartment, and my brother made eggs and coffee while we were all in a thick haze. Although we talked about the dignity of her death and the amazing timing with us all being present, the words were a thin shell of protection against the emotional chaos going on inside each of us. No one can understand that part, and Ken's presence would have thickened that veneer, and veneer is not substance. When your mother dies, everything is about the substance of your lifelong relationship with her.

When I came home later that morning, Ken put his arms around me and just held me. I felt loved and cared for. Not a lot of talk. There was not much to say.

CHAPTER 9

THE ROLE OF FRIENDS

It was in this area, with my friends—that there was tremendous power in sharing my feelings with words.

The single biggest downside to moving from the apartment in the Bronx that I had called home for 20 years was the loss of the intimate relationship with the friends I had around me throughout that time.

My friends knew me before my divorce; we raised our children together. They knew my parents' involvement in my life—weathering the storm of my ups-and-downs, their ups-and-downs. I had intimate friends, friends of 20 years duration at home and at work.

This was my social network. They all knew about me—my relationship with my son, my parents, the process of adjusting to divorce, the process of meeting someone new, the art of juggling life.

I cannot describe the sense of support I felt as emails poured in, the telephone rang; cards with lengthy notes were received. These were all people who had been a part of my life—both as my son's mother, and as my parent's daughter, for many, many years. And, often, they had experienced such a loss themselves. When I cried on the phone, or talked about "the fog" or talked about the lessons I had been learning from the whole journey, I felt that they really understood. And, feeling really understood is a foundation of emotional stability.

But, you must let people know. If your circle of friends and acquaintances are not aware of the loss, they can't be there for you. It can be very painful to call people, or email to let them know that you have lost someone close to you, but the effort will come back to you tenfold.

When my mother died, the first series of phone calls went out to *her* friends. My brother did that. We went through her (many) phone books and checked with my father as to whom we would actually call. That happened while we were still at my father's house, preparing for a memorial that my brother and his wife held for all my parents' friends back in New York.

When I got back to my house, the first round of calls went to my most intimate friends.

The second round of contact was one of emails to all the people in my neighborhood in New York that I would see at least once a week. When I lived in New York, my community-based practice had been very active, so the people with whom I had worked, often for many years, were an important part of my ongoing life experience. My conversations with them all were extremely helpful since so many had experienced such a loss themselves and could share their feelings.

The next group of people in my life with whom I shared news of my mother's death was several very close friends at the social service agency I had worked at for 17 years. And as many of you also know, there are circles of acquaintance in your professional life as well as your social life. When I left my agency in Westchester to move to Michigan, I was given a lovely goodbye party. I asked my parents to come to this party—I had told them all the stories over my 17 years of tenure there. They knew my history with senior administration and my colleagues and were able to share in the good wishes that met me as I left the agency. That goodbye party turned out to be one of the most beautiful opportunities to say goodbye in my life, but to the point here, many of my colleagues as well as the executive director had met my parents, so their condolences carried a different kind of weight. One of my close friends at work had put out an agency-wide bereavement notice, which I would never have thought of doing. That gesture was a lovely gift to me and reminded me that during the immediate time after the death of a loved one, one of the most valuable things that someone can do for you is take on the task of informing others.

Their support will come back to you and make a huge impact on how you process the emotions you feel over the next year or so.

Don't be put off if you haven't spoken to an old friend for years. Often, it is these people who knew you at an earlier time in your life who will really relate to who your mother was ... because they knew her.

As we all know, friends are different than life partners. And it is only fair that our expectations reflect that difference. Accept the way that each person supports you as his or her own individual gift—it may be a big gift, it may be a small one, but you may be surprised by how much of their inner self they are sharing with you.

CHAPTER 10

COMING OUT OF THE FOG

You know, every chapter came to my mind within three weeks of my mother's death—except this last chapter.

I had absolutely no preparation for the pervasive confusion, inability to focus, disorientation, and overall malaise that I would feel for many months after my mother's death. And, although concern for my father, working through administrative issues at the retirement community, resolving banking crises were part of the overall picture, I must say that these logistical issues had nothing to do with my emotional state.

In fact, exactly the opposite.

Whereas the primary emotion that I struggled with while walking through my mother's end of life with her was feeling overwhelmed, the primary emotion I felt following her death was emptiness.

Like an emotional pre-Bing Bang quark soup.

I couldn't put my priorities in order. I couldn't organize my thinking. I messed up time schedules and appointments. Everything on the fringe around my mother's life and death were ... vague.

I must say, this was totally unexpected. My greatest stabilizer in her old age was my focus on task completion and attention to detail. The Solace of Action. But, following her death, I felt a total inability to "make way" to "move forward" ... for months.

I was not overwhelmed by grief in her passing. I shared as much as I could with my mother, she was fairly healthy until the end of her life, she was cognitively clearer than I was, and she did not suffer long. I was not racked by anger, guilt, and a sense of injustice or fear.

But I was consumed by upsetting touchstones, waves of upset, and emptiness. The upset was worse at night, and the emptiness and confusion worse during the day. I felt that I was trying very hard to walk one step through the fog during my waking hours. It did not feel like a cloud over my head, it felt like walking through a cloud. One of my valued friends talked about feeling the loss at a cellular level and I think that is true. Whatever quantum physics framework ties us all together—one generation to the next—there is a very deep sense of loss—a vacuum sucked out of your inner self—that is experienced when you lose a parent.

The process of self-retrieval is gradual. Personally, it took me about three months to feel like I was able to function in the world again—chart a course, clarify personal priorities, organize my thinking ... without merely going through the motions. Ironically, writing this book did not organize me. It has been allowing me to walk a very narrow path through the fog—carrying it's own direction.

It has allowed me to consider the lessons that I have learned through this developmental stage in my life—a stage that so many of us face. Just like all the developmental challenges that we face though our lives—entering school, facing adulthood, parenting ... don't back away. Walk through ... you can't jump over.

Life doesn't let you.

Nor does death.

The sun will come out. The disorientation will diminish—although at this writing, not completely fade. Know that you tried your very best.

Taking in the lessons of walking hand in hand through the end of life with someone you love will continue to unfold. It will let you say goodbye with love and respect.

And, ultimately, this is the goal for us all.

ABOUT THE AUTHOR

Terry Lanigan, LMSW, ACSW received her Master's Degree in Social Work from the University of Chicago. She is a licensed Master's Social Worker in the State of Michigan and is a member of the Academy of Certified Social Workers. Terry has an extensive background in the delivery and supervision of psychotherapy services.

Ms. Lanigan currently maintains a private psychotherapy practice in Grand Haven, Michigan. She can be reached through her website, www.terrylanigan.com.

Additional resources and consulting services are available through www.agingwithsupport.com.

My mother, Edith Bronner

September 18, 1921 – January 19, 2009

Made in the USA
Charleston, SC
02 January 2012